WATCHING FOR SIGNS

First published in 2005 by
Dedalus Press
13 Moyclare Road
Baldoyle
Dublin 13
Ireland

www.dedaluspress.com

© Ann Joyce & Dedalus Press, 2005

All rights reserved. No part of this publication may be reproduced in any form or by any means without the prior permission of the publisher.

ISBN 1 904556 36 1 (paper)
ISBN 1 904556 37 X (bound)

Dedalus Press titles are represented and distributed in the USA and Canada by Dufour Editions Ltd., PO Box 7, Chester Springs, Pennsylvania 19425, and in the UK by Central Books, 99 Wallis Road, London E9 5LN.

Front cover image by Michael Boran.

Printed in Ireland by ColourBooks.

The Dedalus Press receives financial assistance from An Chomhairle Ealaíon / The Arts Council, Ireland.

Contents

Beyond the Bay	1
Land Woman	2
Are You Settled Now?	3
Silk	4
The Freedom of It	6
September Orchard	7
Ripened Fruit	8
A Wish for my Father	9
A Proper Time	10
The Fields above the Crossroads	11
The Tramp	12
Sherry Ladies	14
Frybrook House	15
The Lacemakers	16
Conversation with a Sod of Turf	18
Mid-Winter	19
Heading West	21
Keelogues	22
I Will Always See You There	27
My Mother is Arranging Everything	28
The Long Whisper	30
Sea Walking	31
Woman of Dark Water	32
November Day	33
It is Ordained	34
Emigrant	35
Sky Watching	36
Knockmina	37
The Visit	39
The Meadow	40
Buttermilk Clean	41
Her Six Sons Carried Her	42
Uncle Jimmy	43

Wings	44
Fallen Silence	45
So What do I Leave my Children?	46
January at Rosses Point	49
The Ploughing Championship at Coney Island	50
I Would Ask of You	52
The Bend in the River	53
The Blue Bowl	54
Dream	55
On Sundays and Holydays	56
What I Remember	59
Leningrad Woman	60
A House in Amsterdam	61
Turbulence	62

In memoriam Joseph Mannion

Beyond the Bay

The bay opens its doors
    to liners, yachts, boats;
        houses staring out to sea.

Women watch the tides
    ebb and flow,
        windows of the moon.

They dream rooms
    are ships, moving
        towards horizons and beyond.

Wild sea, without
    gate or wall,
        gathers them into its swell.

Land Woman

The land woman has travelled to the sea,
to the smell of salt in her nostrils,
to a shore of seaweed, shell, stones.

Behind her, the flaking edges of a walled town,
specks of paint caught in her coat
as she pulled the door shut.

She will shake them free
before the Atlantic breeze,
watch them disappear.

She will wipe clean handprints,
smudged shadows of lives left behind,
make her own imprint, however temporary.

Her feet sink into sand.
In a day her footsteps will have gone,
everything fallen into the song,

the light and the night
of the water's embrace,
into the rift and stride of tide.

The sea measures time,
gathers to itself a boat
abandoned in the bay.

Mussel shells at her feet,
the land woman has arrived
at where the sea begins.

Are You Settled Now?

The grass
has not been cut.
Seed heads burst
and scatter on the wind.
Summer hasn't come.
Rainstorm. The sky so close
she might touch it.

The sea swells around her.
Wind blows her back
to the limestone quarry
where goats walk the edge.
One topples from the brim,
hits the rocks below.
A dog barks.

Which would you prefer?
her neighbours ask,
here or …
They have forgotten
where she came from.

The sea moves out,
the shore breathes again,
the quarry gathers the evening.
Are you settled now?

She takes a stone in her hand,
feels its awkward shape,
lays it down again
to find its own place.

Silk

The swap-shop window
in the High Street
opposite the undertakers
is filled with remnants
of something, of everything, of nothing.
The shapes of all women are here
behind glass, rebuilt, reinvented.

The black and white hand-knit cardigan
buttoned to the neckline,
solid as my grandmother
who ordered all the days,
and there, at the side,
behind the tweed suit,
the silk blouse, blue as oceans...

Breeze skims my face,
street lights move a mile
and I hear the clinking glasses,
laughter, indiscernible voices.

A breath of smoke is blown
through painted lips and the ash
on the cigarette wavers.

Envelopes of nights
sealed and put away.
I want to take them out,
wear them, feel silk next to my skin,
sheer as warm seas.

I want to shed this cardigan,
this closed door, weathered
like my grandmother's face.
I want to wear this party,
this light threading the High Street,
this silk thread that makes my body dance.

The Freedom of It

Regardless of how blind my window is
there is always a fragment of light
to seek out the cob-webbed corner
of my room, to paint it golden.

I open the curtain on a sea of stories,
recollections opening like daisies:
climbing a hill in Mayo, only to roll down again
for the sheer freedom of it,

damming a stream with stones and fists of earth
in the hope that salmon, spawning
in the Moy will seek out the ordinary,
risk the journey upstream.

This morning, like so many mornings now,
becomes whatever I want it to be.
For the sheer freedom of it, I take
whatever comes, then let it go.

September Orchard

The orchard is filled with trees,
their boughs laden with apples
that hang like corpses.

In the corner beside the blue house
trunks of dead elms stand
like ceremonial guards on duty.

Stillness creeps everywhere
and I stop my hand
from plucking the red fruit,

as if any disturbance
would be sacrilege
in this hour of natural fall.

Ripened Fruit

Each September the same gossip
moves through the orchard
like crows in a field of stubble,
the last stories and conversations
between apple and elderberry.

Days shorten with every turn of sun.
We walk the worn path to winter:
the crunch of feet on gravel,
my daughter's hand in mine,
ripened fruit mirrored in her face.

A Wish for My Father

When you have drawn your last pipe
and the smoke has risen, dissipated,
and you cradle your meerschaum with cupped hands
close to your heart,

let it be by the river
where eels once danced out of reach
and wild gorse stopped in its path
bowing before your sickle.

Let the scent of meadowsweet
be your incense, and the breeze
blowing through trees
carry you gently off through your fields.

Let stones salute you,
witness to your working hands,
and may the sunset, wild in its dying,
walk out with you through the gates of night.

A Proper Time

The ceiling shimmers. Shadows dance.
Tinsel stars and angels swing together.
Pictures are framed with holly,
clusters of red berries, watching, alert.
The kitchen is invaded by waifs
rehearsing the pantomime drama
as the room fills with music.

In the sick-room
my father sleeps,
frail body smaller now.
At times, his hands grab the air.
Does the children's laughter reach him?

I am a stranger
drowned in his mind.
Sometimes I surface
and he smiles
then loses me again.

I count his breaths, watch
wrinkles soften in his skin.
The carol singers pause for breath.
I want more of him.

The Fields Above the Crossroads
after a painting by Maria Simmons-Gooding

In vivid greens,
without hedges, trees or fences,
she's painted the fields.

Paths of silver grey,
like my father's hair, move
in bends and straights through them.

I know every inch
of these fields. My hands have combed
every blade of grass, collected

every withered wisp,
built haystacks of stories,
stored others away.

And I know too the other painted field,
the field with the awkward shape,
the one with the many sides

and the six white stones
that grow up out of the earth;
my hands live in those stones too.

The Tramp

He came to our village each summer,
jabbed at our conscience,
disturbed our settled ways,
slept in our sheds.

His voice, fierce as a gale,
shook the hedges as he walked past.
People scampered in all directions,
dogs chased him, pitchforks
were brandished behind him,
mothers threatened children
with his name.

My father befriended him,
told me stories
of a homeless boy with a spirit
wild as the flaming whin
reared by strangers.

I wanted to see him,
this traveller of the roads.
I watched for his coming,
searched for signs,
found the shed where he slept,
a hollow in an armful of hay.

We startled each other,
trespassers both of us,
he with his bread and his eggs
stolen from my neighbour's shop,
me, a curious eight year old,
not sure of what I was looking for –

some notion, the wonder
of a story, a whiskered face,
a smile breaking through...
We sat together eating apples
from my father's orchard,
two rogues, delighted with life.

Sherry Ladies

At Nutwell Nursing House
antique ladies sip sherry at eleven,
eye each other from under coifed hair,
laugh softly between practised conversations.
When the doctors come
they sink into chairs,
moan and sigh and point to pain
in their withered skin, then swallow
medicinal syrup from china cups.

At four in the afternoon,
as the sun streams through tall windows,
they breathe deeply into smoke-stained lungs,
stare into scented cards before them,
gold pens poised like cigarettes
in their painted mouths,
and try to remember friends.

But at night,
alone in railed-up beds,
their finery discarded on steel chairs,
they whimper into starched pillows.

Frybrook House

They left their ships at home and steered instead
a sea of multicoloured thread through looms,
where designs danced each day to weaver's tunes.
Skilled hands stretched and played the wool
to build with bricks of cloth a house of dreams.

Within the high-walled garden plot at dusk
the roof-top bell called all of them to dine
at polished tables laid with silver smiles.
Ringed fingers raised the claret cup
while sentry rooks in sycamore crowns looked on.

The house is worn, its edges frayed with time,
disguising smiles of boys and girls who play
at hide and seek among the tattered trees.
The beat of hooves still echoes through the fields
and foxes doze, sensing the chase is done.

Chimneys peep between the trees and rest
while ovens, tired from baking bread, sleep on.
They dream of ships and sails and weaving thread
through waves of rushing water, listening
to broken footsteps fading through closed gates.

The Lacemakers

On the museum stand
a piece of antique lace;
petals torn,
stitched hearts laid bare,
stems and branches broken.

Bread for lace, women
appease the hunger.
Eyes focus on white mesh
held taut by timber hands.

Needles steer thread
through veins of cracked ice,
make trails of flowers
gliding over fingers,
over high stone walls

into the big houses
where ruffles swirl,
silk skirts spin,
and lace dances
on polished wood.

Churches open their oak doors,
bolts of lace unfurl
to dress priests and altars
in transformed thread.

Women kneel in pews,
their faces creased with patterning,
listening for the flicker of light,
their eyes blinded for lace
and hands outstretched for bread.

Conversation with a Sod of Turf

And tell me, that day
when the clean sharp sleán
cut into your mother's flesh
did your cries echo in the April day?

And tell me, were they stifled
by the yearning of men
who would watch you burn
like a witch at the stake?

Or was this day your dream,
your prayer, your epiphany,
the wind drying years of tears
that had languished in dark earth?

Mid-Winter

The man in the grey tweed jacket
crosses the Blue Bridge over the Coose river,
then turns right, heading for the mountain,
sudden with the urge to look again—

the house white against skeletal trees,
the mud-filled path,
the turf shed with its blind eyes.

Two horses stand where once a hedge
made separate spaces. Fields are lost to water,
the grant-aided fence, the stone wall,
nothing to hold in now....

Clumps of rush reclaim their place,
Cladonia—lime green lichen—
splashing the tired grass.
He wants to go back there, pay homage.

He remembers it all,
the day he first tasted boxty;
relations back from England,
The People newspaper handed round

among the adults only, the day
his grandfather died, the man
who always had nails in his pockets,
the man who took him up the mountain

in a pony and cart collecting the gravel
that would build the shed.

Voices whisper from the haggard.
He sees himself pulling out
newly sewn cabbages for no other reason
than that they gave easily in his small hands.

Sitting on a stone in the centre of the stream,
hands rowing water to catch fish
that have long since abandoned it,
the stream in flood, his aunt and grand-mother

searching, calling, distraught.
Spilling rationed tea leaves
onto the kitchen floor, sweeping them up
into shapes... sweet scent of those leaves.

That living he craves now, outside the stone wall,
looking down into mirroring windows,
a white horse on the other side
steadying his gaze on the mountain.

Heading West

Prayers said, her soul cleansed,
arms folded over her chest,
she let herself out of that place,
headed west along the Swinford road,
her feet light as lace, entered the house
where she was always queen, climbed
the stairs to the bedroom to look
through that glass again, bare branches
of sycamore reaching for sky,
the river hushed in its moving
and beyond, that place her husband
waits as she waited evenings for him
to bring home news of the world.

Keelogues

Everything was warm then,
stones, feathers, bones,
black mud of a pond bed
easy on the hands that shaped it
into rounded cakes, jewelled
with the white seeds
of reeds growing out of water.
Mud-cakes set to bake
then cut open to the core.

That bowl of dug earth:
disused sand pit, my brothers
and friends crouched low inside, sharing
a packet of Sweet Afton.

Wisps of smoke rising
over blackthorns,
the curl of it, secret boys' talk
taking off into the blue
arms of sky.

My father filling his pipe,
handing it to my brother,
telling him *Pull hard.*
My brother, face
bulging, afraid
to swallow, afraid
to open his mouth.

Somewhere I am always going home,
returning to that piece of ground
in the hope that nothing has changed:
the pond, the hand-made dam,
passing trains, the scent of meadowsweet.

The widow woman kneeling
in the middle of the road, hands tearing
her long hair, cursing my father
for grazing the teacher's garden.

Father telling me this story, and more...
I enter the dream of him.
The heat from the kitchen fire,
mushrooms toasting on red coals

until he lifts them on a spoon
like some exotic delicacy,
juice spilling, the best part lost.

What do I want there,
a history
attached to me like a shadow?

The shapes of fields with walls
of drains beneath them, trenches
lined with gathered stones,

and rain seeping through
to find a road to the sea.
Underground maps my grandfather
made with pick-axe and spade.

I have become a journey-woman
following lines on a map.
So much discarded:
my sister's coat, my cousin's dress.
So much taken with me;
my mother's shoes, the friend
who taught me how to paint red peonies.

I stop, look again at the railway track
where children lay down six-inch nails
on its face for the trains
to crush into new shapes.
I walk this iron road,
sensing danger, loving it,
hungry for everything here.

I Will Always See You There

Mother, I will always see you there,
head bent, face stern in concentration,
hands that cannot hold still.
They move with an urgency as if they know
day will end and night is close
with all its darkness.

You found a way of dealing with the night;
your fingers sewed a quilt of lives,
dark and light patched, blended together.
And, though the colours have faded,
the thread still holds, the stitches
still firm as your faith.

Now you have your beads,
large wooden beads blessed in Knock
you pray over each and every day
in your leather chair, the fire at your side,
your window, a drama of sky
and sycamore leaves,
your night, a safe distance away.

My Mother is Arranging Everything

The white table linen
wrapped in tissue paper
in the strawberry scented drawer
for over sixty years
is moving house,

as is the blue and gold dinner service,
the tureens, the china cups with the red stripe,
the nickel-silver cruet set
with its cut-glass jars
that still hold a hint of spice.

My mother is arranging everything.
There will be no scramble for her treasures,
no picking and choosing our own keepsakes.
She will not be forgotten
in the bequests made and the ones hoped for.

My mother is arranging everything.
The prayers for the sick,
the anointing with holy oil,
the hymns during mass and the grand-daughter
who would sing them.

She is wearing the clothes from the hospital bag,
breathing life into them.
The room fills with the scent of camphor.
And in the green bag lying in the wardrobe,
the makings of another journey—
navy blue suit, cream blouse, stockings.

When I see the white gloves I chuckle
as if where she is going will be cold,
and those navy shoes of hers will beat a path
as far away as possible from the heat
she cannot abide.

She has taken to cycling now
in her nightly ramblings, talking about trips
around Breaffy, Ballyheane, Milebush,
and I follow her every wheel-turn,
dodging briars and overgrown blackthorns
while the grey sky threatens to smother me,
heavy as delft. I take
her hand in mind. It is still warm.

The Long Whisper

Today the river stopped flowing.
Drought reached my soul.

Wind stood on the hill top,
shaped you into statue.

Now, grass is on fire.
I stand at the fence-post, seeing nothing.

Soil is turned over.
I stumble in fresh earth.

I pick a rose from a bush,
petals white like your face.

Today I listen to a long whisper
carry you off on a broken wing.

Sea Walking

I can always accept the roaring waves
offering themselves to a waiting shore,
can accept the strength
of what the sea is.

It is the silent water I dread,
the calm, barely moving water
that lulls me into the mistaken belief
that I might walk across its floor.

Woman of Dark Water

Old woman,
crouched behind
shuttered windows,
hiding from footsteps
and passing shadows.

Old woman
of dark water,
the tide breaks
against the barrier wall
but your door
remains shut.

Old woman,
in your wild skirts,
in your tide skirts,
the ebb and flow of centuries
spilling over you,

trawling our nights,
our sleepless nights,
you are the keeper
of our shadows.

November Day

This November day, still
as a picture postcard,
the sky ice-blue,
the sea holding its breath.
I dig furiously,

replanting daffodils
from their temporary verge
beside the vegetable plot,
bulbs carried in Spring
from my mother's garden,
across county boundaries.

In this unnatural stillness
I keep moving, urging the earth
to stay awake, to fear the fate
of the sleeping princess.

It is Ordained

The leaves will always fall; *it is ordained,*
so cut that line, no need to sing its praise
and rain will lash the trees with pure disdain.

It does not matter, she will not be named,
her pen dispatches lines into a blaze.
The leaves will always fall; it is ordained.

Smiles from whiskered faces must not remain
but *land women travelling to the sea* stays
and rain will lash the trees with pure disdain.

My parlour lines, my poems in tatters, drained
of *and* and *the,* stitch words - erase, erase!
The leaves will always fall; it is ordained.

Stanzas stripped and bruised in battle, blood-stained,
they stand their ground, continue to amaze
and rain will lash the trees with pure disdain.

Cut the comment, simplify! I'll be dammed
if she with pencil forces a rephrase.
The leaves will always fall; it is ordained
and rain will lash the trees with pure disdain.

Emigrant

Standing against the stark white wall
shoulders hunched, he stares
into the eye of the camera,
a man facing a firing squad,
listens for the click
that transforms him into an image
to fit the allotted space on the page.
Strands of sandy hair fall
over his forehead, past his eyes,
shield him from the thump
of the rubber stamp
in the passport office.

Sky Watching

After mass she took the lift
to the eleventh floor, close to the sky,
to the blue that settles over Central Park
as if someone had brushed everything
sharp and clean and true.

Tree tops level with her,
bare branches scattered in jigsaw shapes.
Were the walls not here to hold her
she would imagine them.

She would scatter her pictures here,
let them drift one by one into the blue
mingle of cloud, tree, earth:

the cottage, its space of rooms
folding her days into packets;
pockets of fields neatly lined
with cowslip and buttercup;
a frame of dry-stone walls;
the small American flag
posted for visitors.

They would scatter and drift,
even the most difficult of them—Lough Arrow
where Barry used to fish.

In her own time she would walk
down the flight of stairs,
steadying herself on the way,
to feel a Manhattan pavement
solid underfoot.

Knockmina

"*Very tall, very thin, very black,
the best cornbread baker in all Selma...*"
You tell me about Anna,
the Underdonk's maid,
her hair wrapped in a purple and orange
flour-sack turban, her one-roomed shack
papered with pictures from magazines
and mail-order catalogues.

I tell you about white-thorn—
a marker for famine graves,
unlucky if taken indoors—
how once, not knowing the story,
I placed a branch in a vase on the window
and my mother waited days, checking for mishaps,
the white blossom falling slowly.

We talk of magnolia,
rope swings, walnut groves,
summers watching apples ripen.
Stories traded, settling themselves
like stones in a nest of grass.

You said you'd take them with you
to the cotton farms of Alabama.

Now day drains of light,
swallows twitch on telephone wires,
prepare for the journey south.
The sky fills with paint-box colour.
A limestone wall crumbles,
ivy creeps along its face,

a white-thorn sprouts at its feet,
every day resurrection.
It doesn't matter
whether great thoughts rise
from this evening.
It is enough we are here,
two women, making conversation,
at a roadside in Knockmina,
stirring white days into night.

The Visit

Back from America to visit his sister,
he brought a wife, a daughter,
a life he carried inside of him.
He wanted to show them everything:

the lilacs in the teacher's garden,
branches torn taking home an offering,
the scent that filled the kitchen, mixing
with burning paraffin oil;

horse chestnut trees round that bend
on the road where the daft woman lived,
pockets full of conkers, strings of them,
made into whistles, catapults, slings;

the ball alley, white-washed gable
of the shopkeeper's barn, summer evenings
stepped out to the babel of feet, hands
and hard-ball, grunts of stretched muscle;

the straight piece of road, circle marked
with chalk, skittles set out, the wall
where the girls sat watching,
that world he could not let go.

In the photograph they stand
in the middle of the road,
the daughter in white summer dress
the father in black double-breasted suit...

That space between them...
You could build a wall,
day on one side,
night on the other.

The Meadow

My mother asks me to cut her hair
straight, like the first sward of meadow.
This is the way she wants it, this expert
of directness, this woman from Mayo
who refuses to bend or curve or lose herself
in a grey maze of tangled hair.
I want to layer it, toss it, turn it, choose
to curl this silken skein, this fine coiffure.

And then I see her, a meadow: foxglove,
grasses, burrs and seed-heads, ripened somehow,
ready for fall. Her locks stagger and bend,
my hand starts to cut, caught in a headwind.

Buttermilk Clean

He married a woman returned from America.
She bore him children, rested in the mornings,
took naps in the afternoons, dreamed of orange blossom.

He took care of the house, savoured the whiteness of it,
lime-white of the walls, flour-white of his hands,
bleached his freckles, creamed his face soft, buttermilk clean.

When he climbed the ladder to brush the chimney
the black soot crept out over his arms,
filled the pores of his skin, shadowed the blue of his eyes.
His heart went into shock, stood still.

Her Six Sons Carried Her

Her six sons carried her on their shoulders
the length of the cemetery,
circled the ruined church,
bent their heads under the arched window,
touched the earth the saint had blessed,
tightened their grip in the path of tradition,
then doubled back to the mound of brown earth
bedecked with palms and roses...
And as they lowered her into the grave
they saw the dust, that was once their father, dance.

Uncle Jimmy
for Cathal Ó Searcaigh

My uncle Jimmy fell from a scaffold
in Westport and became a surrealist.

He would walk the roads, his blackthorn stick
beating flies from hedges.

"Sins," he would shout, "the lot of them,"
black sins eating his days until everything

became night, shouts of sin that carried through
open windows to startled children.

Days, he was a general leading battalions
in the French Foreign Legion,

his stick, a sword routing enemies
from flower formations in our neighbours' gardens.

When all was a battlefield, he would sing
about an Irishman shining in the sky.

I searched the clouds for this man of light
drawing plaintive notes through space.

My mother made him currant cakes,
fed him thick slices buttered with fried bacon.

On quiet evenings, gathering wind-blown apples,
he would feel the clay, let it fall through his fingers,

tell me that he himself was clay, his skin
a white shell encasing the black soil of despair.

Wings

I watch birds:
swallows returning to the barn,
robins at my feet whenever
I dig fresh earth, thrushes
stalking worms in the wet grass.

I am reminded of the woman
who passed her days feeding
rooks and crows with bread
hoarded in plastic bags;

how she waited beside the sycamore
for the movement of birds,
the tremor of branch or wing,
their raucous singing
after the old man died.

When her neighbour talked
of felling the tree, for fear of it falling
in a winter storm, she cried
at another anticipated loss,
her prayers louder than the din
of birds on the slates.

My nights are filling now
with sleeping birds, shadow-women and trees.
Breadcrumbs scattered on the table,
I move them about, finger them,
shape crusts into wings and wait
for the swoop of rooks.

Fallen Silence

There, in the fallen silence
is the place I go to, the place I invent,
everything rounded, thorns shed,
berries red as wet paint in an open tin.

I fall into meadowsweet and half-light,
the touch of skin on skin,
whispers of what was then love.
I fall into the wet dew of childhood

drawn back to the mountain,
my name sewn into its quilted coat,
threading me into walls, broken-down gaps
I move through on a thought.

Even disasters are bearable there.
I spread them out as I would a creel of turf,
let the wind and sun give them new skin
lighten the weight of their bodies.

In my father's fields, the shape
of his hands lingers in ditches.
Grass stirs. The gap in the hawthorn hedge
opens in and out.

So What Do I Leave My Children?

I'm home from a walk
and you ask where I've been.
I tell you I have gone back
to the place you cannot enter
to the back room,

the *you are too young* room,
the *what do you know?* room
the *you're only a girl* room.
I find my shape there.
No sense to it at all.

This room that still shadows
the edge of my breathing,
a room of *thou shalt not,*
of *sins against everything.*

Deadly sins numbered and learned,
mortal sins that leave me dammed,
pain and loss and fear...
Eternity is too long, longer
than the flow of the stream reaching
for the Atlantic.

So what do I leave my children,
the gift of forgetting?

When you ask where I come from
I tell you, I am from Mayo,
from the aching back of a turf bog,
from the dark waters of a pond
that coughed me up
onto a bed of reeds.

I tell you I am from
things broken and things fixed,
the stream eager in its run,
wells I left behind me,
my son's dying,
my children's tears...

So what do I leave my children?

Before me, fields,
mottled meadow, gorse, rush,
ground
wild with bog-cotton;

a stippled sky more true
than a Paul Henry painting.
I measure my steps against these skies
let the fire of sunset lift me.

I walk a road
that once was a running stream,
talk into fields of corn,
measure time
in the colour of their skin.

So what can I leave my children?
Wild strawberries run
red beneath the hedge.
I taste them again.
The sweetness passes like flights
of starlings in an autumn evening.

January at Rosses Point

Brown ducks swim into the wind
cutting through water
like scissors through cloth.
Ridges of waves are blown
from the confines of the channel
to prospect in the wider ocean.

The air is clean, washed down
by white cloths of snow.
Earth wakens from dream stirrings
in its dark body.
In beds nestling under cover of hebe
snowdrops probe the daylight.

Along the promenade, walkers
with arms like wings
stride into the New Year,
their footsteps a definite
beat in the symphony
of water, duck song
and the solo barking of a dog.

Through the open shop door
over-ripe bananas selling at half price
make me forget winter has ever been.
Resolution urges me to admire again
nesting in the bank of rocks
the first wild valerian green.

The Ploughing Championship at Coney Island

The car moves through shallows of water,
a row of pillars, markers for the journey.
A flush of sea anemones
unafraid of salt in their nostrils
creep at will over sands
the sea claws cannot reach.
The gloom of the mainland fades.

The island waits like an unhurried summer.
Content in its position,
everything around it shifts,
moves out, doubles back, forever in motion.
The day takes my hand, walks with me.

Sand sweeps before me,
the earth turns,
rows of earth filled with the scent of sea.
Tractors inch forward,
plough blades cut the sod
sharp and clean, edges neat and uniform.

The farmer's eye trained straight,
the dream in each turn of head.
Levers are moved, screws turned,
blades lifted and dropped, weights added,
the earth moves.

Women and children in the field,
men turning the earth,
the ripples of ancestors.

Everything is a door,
touch stones, push them open,
find memory in the crevice.
Catch thoughts and hold them
before they run
with the yellow of yarrow,
the purple of thistle,
the strength of bleached marram.
Everything is alive.

Houses squat, defiant,
wanting a piece of this landscape.
On walls, on half-hedges,
young men sit drinking black porter.
Everyone stops here.

I search for connection,
find it in the blown kiss
of wind on my face,
a fistful of warm clay, brown
earth ploughed open.

I Would Ask of You

I would ask of you
only sky, shift of cloud,
blue strip of wit you let go
on days I need it most.

Sometimes I live under stairs,
dark places without door or window.
Walls of black as if someone
had painted them over and over
increasing the depth.

At those times I think of you—
a white gull, flight in your wings—
and you have me in stitches
with stories light as air,

sea smoke rising, moving out beyond
Drumcliff bay, an ocean at your fingertips,
the bright reason of your being
blazing the dark.

The Bend in the River

As a woman might carry a shoulder-bag, I carry
that morning I stepped out of the green jeep,
walked towards the bank of the Nam Xong River,
out over mud and stones to where the long boats
were moored, measured the water with my eyes,
the bend in the river where the water turned
and in that turning saw swirling beneath the surface
the place where it all began, the place
I will spend my life making sense of.

The Blue Bowl

The hand-thrown bowl is filled
with hand-picked stones
from the edge of the Nam Xong river.

Surely his feet must have touched them,
hot from October sun, the rounded shapes
printing his soles as he moved;

and if not, then his shadow must have cast itself
along the verge of water and mud,
spread out like a coat;

and if not, his breath rowing
through currents must have fallen
on them, light as the notes of a song;

and if not, the water that took him
to itself like a precious gem
must have lapped gently over them

knowing I would come to find them.

Dream

I want to spread you out
among red peonies,
grow you there in the well of them,
watch the curl of you open out
from the crimson womb
to live another life.

On Sundays and Holy Days...

She prayed,
forty days of Lent,
six weeks of Advent,
sodality days every month.
Refused meat on Fridays,
afraid of hell, of losing her God,
her picture on the wall,
her statue of chalk.

Made pilgrimages to Knock,
lit candles, recited litanies,
novenas, the Thirty Days Prayer,
knelt for rosaries,
knees on cement floors,
arms draped in the crucifix
of a wooden chair.

She prayed,
preparing station breakfasts—
poached eggs, fresh grapefruit,
dissected, de-seeded, purified,
cube sugar, cream, currant bread—
told stories of sins committed,
for mercy she prayed.

Her skin wrinkled like corrugated paper,
she demanded to be taken care of,
pulled down a blind on every day,
slumped in an armchair.

Unsure of whose house she was in
childhood dangled before her.
Family became strangers,
she re-christened them,
called out names like a school roll,
everyone someone else.

When television spewed out news
of a murder trial she drew closer,
shushed all around her, believed
the woman on trial was a school friend,
laughed at that old audacity,
said she hadn't changed a bit.

And she sewed:
into a pouch worn round her neck
scapulars and miraculous medals,
and in the buttonhole of her nightgown
a knot of rosary beads.

Sundays and Holy days
prayers spill out from behind
the wallpaper in the day-room.
Spaces filled with sacred music,
she joins in a verse of a hymn
"Faith of our fathers, living still."

What I Remember

Who can remember the first year
let alone the first hour? All I can do
is imagine myself swimming in a bubble

round and round inside my mother,
my body curled like a fist, my mother
doing time, counting months, then days.

A summer baby, the wild pain,
room bristling with birth-cries.
You get used to it, this gift of child.

I imagine I drooled over her summer
dress, the small daisy print my earth,
holding tight to myself that small part

of self I could never let go, not even
to her warm arms nestling me,
holding me as she would a china cup.

What I do remember is my mother
standing at the table by the window,
the oil lamp hanging above her

like her off-centre halo,
my hands holding the sides
of a cradle my father had fashioned,

singing about going to *Amer-ge-go,*
ready even then to fly the coop.

Leningrad Woman
after a painting by Boris Ugarov

No matter what, he would paint her,
his Leningrad Woman—black hair

scarved, skirt reaching her ankles,
long black jacket, her hands gloved,

just a hint of wrist showing,
and her face, no matter what

he had to share her face, this woman
he wanted for himself, his eyes alone,

standing before him in candle-light
or in the flicker of wood fire.

He wanted to draw his brush across
every piece of her skin, wanted it

with such a passion that having drawn
her shape on canvas he would cover her

with strokes of paint, his hand moving
over every inch of her until he could

bear it no more; then he would place her
outside in the snow, surrounded

by three-storey buildings, grey with hunger,
dragging her sledge through the streets.

A House in Amsterdam

A year later and I want to understand my curiosity,
a stop on a canal trip, stepping from the boat,
queuing in the Amsterdam sun, reading a leaflet,
the history of a house, *"a museum with a story"*,
snippets of a young girl's writing.

What had I come to see – a book-case blocking
a door to a secret world: a young girl reading
from *Cinema and Theatre*, posting pictures
of film stars on the wall, washing herself at a sink,
keeping a diary of war.

Was it not enough to believe the story
without checking the certainty, without putting
my hand on the wall where wounds show?
The word should be enough.

Turbulence

On a plane journey to Cyprus, the screen reads
speed: 600km, altitude: 30,000ft.
The sky is clear; below me, snow-clad mountains.

Strange that I should think of you now, father,
on your scooter, *terra firma*, a September evening,
coming home from work and crashing into the herd of cattle.

It wasn't the drink, nor fog nor anything we knew,
not the grime on your glasses blurring the distance,
black shapes suddenly all about you.

It must have been your mind wandering off to that place
you go to, that hill you stand on looking down
into barley fields when you tumbled headlong,

grazed your face, the knuckles of your right hand.
The doctor's sedative didn't work,
heightened the excitement, sent you into overdrive,

the view from that hill attaching itself to you,
wings and flight and tumbling through the air.
The captain reminding us to fasten our seat belts,

turbulence over the Pindus mountains,
an electrical storm invading our space,
cushions of white snow all around.